The Path to the Throne of God

STUDY GUIDE

by
Grace A. Johnson

Accompainment to Sarah Peck's classic book on the Sanctuary.

World rights reserved. This book or any portion thereof may not be copied or reproduced in any form or manner whatever, except as provided by law, without the written permission of the publisher, except by a reviewer who may quote brief passages in a review.

The author assumes full responsibility for the accuracy of all facts and quotations as cited in this book. The opinions expressed in this book are the author's personal views and interpretations, and do not necessarily reflect those of the publisher.

This book is provided with the understanding that the publisher is not engaged in giving spiritual, legal, medical, or other professional advice. If authoritative advice is needed, the reader should seek the counsel of a competent professional.

Copyright © 2024 Grace A. Johnson

Copyright © 2024 TEACH Services, Inc.

ISBN-13: 978-1-4796-1738-8 (Paperback)

All scripture quotations, unless otherwise indicated, are taken from King James Version. Public domain.

Editor's Note: The book to which this study guide relates, The Path to the Throne of God, was written many decades ago, and thus contains capitalization and spelling that are now outdated. This study guide has replaced "vail" with "veil," dropped extraneous capital letters, etc., to meet current standards.

Chapter 1: *The Sanctuary—One of God's Lesson Books*

1. What are God's three lesson books? _____ _____ _____

2. What is "the grand theme of these books"? _____ _____ ___ _____

3. ... "in our study and teaching of nature, the work of Christ not only as _____ but as _____, is made plain."

4. "Thus, the sanctuary not only illuminates _____, but it reveals _____."

5. When was God's third book, the _____, completed? _____
   _____.

Chapter 2: *The Sanctuary—The Gospel in the Old Testament*

1. Who preached the gospel to Israel? _____ How did he preach it? _____
   _____

2. "Through _____ was to be fulfilled the purpose of which the _____ was a symbol" (Ed 36).

3. Psalm 29:9 (margin) states that "in His _____."

4. What four books comprise "*The Gospel according to Moses*"? On the line beside each book describe the work of salvation that is presented, in type, through Christ.
   a. _____   _____
   b. _____   _____
   c. _____   _____
   d. _____   _____

5. "Through the _____ of the _____ _____, the gospel is presented in _____;
   _____."

Chapter 3: *The Sanctuary—For Special Study in our Day*

1. "A study of the sanctuary contains _____ _____ _____ _____ _____."

2. "At the age of _____, for the first time the child _____ looked upon the _____....
   The _____ of His _____ was opening to the _____" (DA 78).

3. It has been said, "that without a knowledge of _____ _____ 'it will be impossible for them (church members) to exercise _____ _____ which is essential at this time, or to occupy the _____ God designs them to _____'".

4. "The _____ illustrates not only the plan of _____ in general, but it points out the _____ _____ _____ that pertain particularly to _____ _____ _____ and on _____ to the very _____ _____ _____."

5. "In the _____, _____ of every kind is to arise, and we want _____ _____ for our feet. The _____ will bring in _____ _____ that there is _____ _____. This is one of the points on which there will be a _____ from the _____" (Ellen G. White, RH, May 25, 1905).

Chapter 4: *Israel's Preparation for Service*

1. The expression "the selfsame day" refers to two specific time periods. What are those time periods? Give a reference for each. _____
   _____

2. Do you know the song, "The Song of Moses"? _____ Learn it/Sing it and share it with others.

3. On which day of the week did the Israelites leave Egypt, celebrate the First Pentecost, and listen as God spoke His law? _____

4. "The _____ _____ was to be a '_____ of the things in the heavens'" (Heb. 9:23).

5. "On what kind of stone did God write the Ten Commandments"? _____ What was the significance of the color of the stone? _____ _____
   _____

Chapter 5: *"That I May Dwell Among Them"*

1. Write Exodus 25:8. "_____."

2. What is a sanctuary? _____ ____
   _____

3. Write Revelation 21:3. "_____(_____)_____
   _____,_____,
   _____,_____."

Chapter 6: *"Willing-Hearted" Giving*

1. "Our _____ toward _____ _____ determines _____ ____
   _____
   _____."

2. "The _____ has nothing to do with _____ _____."

3. How did the Israelites get their gifts for the sanctuary? _____

Chapter 7: *"Wise-Hearted" Workers "Called"*

1. "God puts _____ in 'all who are _____ _____,' that is, all who from the _____
   _____ their _____ to Him."

2. God's model school was a school in "which the _____, the _____, and the _____, received _____ _____. It was a _____ for all time."

3. "Who giveth thee power to get wealth? Or to do this or that" (Deut. 8:17,18)? _____

4. "Every man also to whom God hath given _____, and _____, and hath given him _____ to _____ thereof, and to take his portion, and to _____ in his _____; this is the _____ _____ _____" (Eccles. 5:19).

5. "There is no _____ to the _____ of one who, putting _____ _____, makes room for the _____ of the _____ _____ upon his heart, and lives a life _____ _____ to God. All who consecrate _____, _____, and _____ to His service will be constantly receiving a new endowment of ____, _____, and _____ power" (MH 159).

Chapter 8: *Christ Entering the Court—This Earth*

1. Where was the promise first given of "Him who would bruise the head of the serpent, the originator of sin"? _____

2. "Finally, the 'fullness of the time was come' (Gal 4:4), when the _____ of the _____ _____ was to enter the _____ _____ _____ _____, when the _____ _____ _____ was to lay aside _____ _____ _____ and _____ and take upon _____ the _____ of _____ flesh."

3. "His true _____ and _____ might have been clearly understood through a _____ understanding of the _____ and the _____."

Chapter 9: *The Christian Entering the Court*

1. What are the three parts of the sanctuary? _____ _____, _____ _____ _____, _____ _____ _____ _____

2. What is represented by each of the sanctuary colors? white: _____ and _____; scarlet: _____; purple: _____; blue: _____.

3. "As the _____ was the way, and the _____ way to the _____ _____, so _____ is the only way to _____."

Chapter 10: *The Court and Its Wall*

1. "The cross of _____, represented in the _____, is the center of _____ life and of the _____ life on _____; the _____, represented in the _____, is the center of _____ _____ in _____ and of the _____ future life in heaven."

2. "Brass signifies _____, _____, _____, and _____ through suffering."

3. "In the _____, silver represents _____ _____ _____."

Chapter 11: *The Brazen Altar*

1. Describe in detail what was on the altar. _____
   Who did it represent? _____

2. "As _____ represented _____, so the _____ as a whole was a symbol of _____ and Him _____."

3. "Christ was treated as we _____, that we might be treated as He _____" (DA 25).

4. "Those who _____ their _____ to His _____ and to His _____ will never be placed in a _____ for which He has not made _____" (MH 248, 249.

5. "The fact that we are called upon to _____ _____ shows that the _____ _____ sees in us something _____, which He desires to _____" (MH 471).

Chapter 12: *The Laver and His Foot*

1. Where was the laver located? _____
   What material was used in the construction of the laver? _____

2. Washing at the laver, corresponded to what two ordinances? _____ and _____

3. "The laver is the complement of the _____; that is, _____, the work begun at the _____, is completed in _____ symbolized at the _____."

Chapter 13: *The Priest and His Garments*

1. How does Exodus 39:27 describe the material of the priests' garments? _____
   _____

2. Of what was this material a symbol? _____

3. "The _____ and _____ of the priests' _____ betokened also the beauty of _____ of every _____ who is an _____ for _____."

4. What are the three orders of priests? _____,
   _____, and _____

Chapter 14: *The Garments of the High Priest*

1. What were on the hem of the High Priest's robe? _____ and
   _____

2. What were engraved on the onyx stones? _____

3. What inscription was engraved on the mitre/holy crown? _____

Chapter 15: *The Heavenly Sanctuary*

1. "The _____ sanctuary is important because it was God's _____ _____ to illustrate _____ in the _____."

2. "Moreover, since the plan of _____ is the '_____ _____ _____' of the Bible, an understanding of both the _____ and the _____ _____ is fundamental to a proper understanding of the _____."

3. "A _____ and _____ picture of the _____ above will enable us to follow _____ where He is now _____ for the _____ of man."

Chapter 16: *Christ Entering the Holy Place of the Heavenly Sanctuary*

1. Which book in the Old Testament of the Bible contains songs about the death, resurrection, and ascension of Jesus? _____

2. What sacred ordinance passed away and what ordinance was instituted by Jesus, "as a memorial of the same event"? _____, _____ _____

3. "When the inauguration of Christ was accomplished, and He began His ministry in the holy place of the heavenly sanctuary," Who did Christ send to His followers? _____ _____ _____

Chapter 17: *The Christian Entering the Holy Place*

1. What does "pressing toward the prize" involve? _____
   _____

2. "_____, obtained in the court, is our _____ into the _____ _____."

3. "While _____--the second birth--is the work of a _____; _____, this 'growing up' process, is the work of a _____, the result of battles fought and victories won."

Chapter 18: *The Sanctuary Wall and Its Floor*

1. How did the height of the sanctuary wall compare to the height of the court walls? _____
   _____

2. What kind of wood was used in the construction of the sanctuary? _____

3. What other materials were used in the building of the sanctuary wall and its floor? _____
   _____.

Chapter 19: *The Four Coverings*

1. What materials made up the four coverings of the roof of the sanctuary? _____
   _____

2. Rams were used in five different types of sacrifices. What were those five types of sacrificial offerings? _____, _____, _____,
   _____ and _____.

3. What are the four division of Christ's redemptive work as represented by the four coverings of the roof of the sanctuary? _____
   _____

Chapter 20: *The Golden Table*

1. "The _____ provides our _____ _____ for _____ growth for _____
   _____ -- for _____."

2. Who is symbolized by the bread on the golden altar? _____ Cite four references from the book of John to support your answer. John _____, John _____, John _____, John _____.

3. What four ingredients were used to make the shewbread? _____, _____, _____, and _____.

Chapter 21: *The Golden Altar*

1. What is the second step in Christian growth? _____

2. Incense was made of what four spices? _____/_____, _____, _____, and
   _____.

3. Why are some prayers not answered? _____
   _____

Chapter 22: *The Candlestick of Beaten Gold*

1. What is the third step in Sanctification/Christian perfection? _____

2. "Why were the ornaments to be made 'like unto almonds'?" _____
   _____

3. "While _____ righteousness frees us from the _____ of our _____, _____ righteousness frees us _____ by _____ from the _____ of sin, and gives us '_____ to become the sons of God' John (____:____)"

Chapter 23: *Christ Entering the Most Holy Place of the Heavenly Sanctuary*

1. What scripture foretold of when Jesus passed within the first veil and was anointed as High Priest? _____ What scripture foretold of when Jesus passed within the second veil to function as Judge? _____

2. When did the last "Time" prophecy begin? _____ What two scriptures mention the "Time of the end," and the "Time appointed"? _____
   What began at the end of the 2,300 days? _____
   What is the historical date for that event? _____

3. What are two of the most important events in the plan of redemption? _____
   _____

4. Who is the Judge? _____

Chapter 24: *The Christian Entering the Most Holy Place*

1. What is our passport into the Most Holy Place? _____

2. What does it mean to "enter within the veil"? _____
   _____

3. What are the other names for the Most Holy Place? _____

Chapter 25: *The Ark and Its Contents*

1. How is the word *ark* defined? _____
   What two other arks are mentioned in the Bible? _____

2. Why has the ark been called God's treasure chest? _____
   _____

3. What three items were placed inside the ark? _____
   _____

Chapter 26: *Mercy Seat and the Shekinah*

1. What is symbolized by the mercy seat? _____

2. Who is represented by the Shekinah? _____

3. What does God's law represent? _____

Chapter 27: *Israel's Day of Atonement and Its Antitype*

1. Why did God instruct the trumpets to be made of silver and "of one whole piece"? _____
   _____
   _____

2. What was the antitype of the most sacred blowing of the trumpets that occurred each year? _____
   _____

   The trumpets were to be blown 10 days before what event? _____
   What date is represented by this ten-day period? _____

3. What were the four definite assignments the people were to follow on the day of atonement?
   _____
   _____

4. "What is it to 'afflict' the soul"? _____
   _____
   Give a scriptural reference to support your answer. _____

5. "There was to be no _____, —the day of _____ demanded _____
   and _____ of every _____."

Chapter 28: *The Judgment and the Sabbath*

1. "The _____ was set apart to be _____ in _____ of God's _____" (EW33).

2. What three items are required for a seal to authorize and validate a document? _____
   _____
   How does the fourth commandment satisfy these three requirements of a seal? _____
   _____.

3. How was God's law preserved and taught? _____
   _____

Chapter 29: *Before the Throne*

1. What are the three books, or sets of books, kept in the heavenly sanctuary? _____
   _____

2. Which do you want blotted out in the heavenly sanctuary's record—sins or names? _____

3. What is heaven's appeal to us today? _____
   _____

Chapter 30: *The Tabernacle Set Up and Anointed*

1. "The _____ so strikingly _____ in all works of God was _____ in the _____
   _____…. At Sinai, the arrangements for _____ were completed" (Ed37).

2. What four sweet spices were contained in the holy anointing oil? _____, _____,
   _____, _____

3. What was the Antitype of "the setting up and anointing of the earthly sanctuary"? _____
   _____

Chapter 31: *The Church of the Court—The Hebrew Church*

1. What are the four "successive 'generations' or divisions" of the church? _____
_____

2. What was the first regularly organized church on this earth? _____

3. What was the first step in the organizing of this church? _____
_____

4. What was the mission of the Hebrew church? _____
_____

Chapter 32: *The Church of the Holy Place—The Christian Church*

1. What was the mission of the Christian church? _____
_____
_____

2. What "was the great burden of the preaching of the apostles"? _____
_____

3. What two events enabled some of the deceptive and destructive errors to be exposed? _____
_____
_____

Chapter 33: *The Church of the Most Holy Place—The Remnant Church*

1. What definition for the word "remnant" is given in Webster's dictionary? _____
_____

2. What warning message was "proclaimed simultaneously by godly men in practically all parts of the civilized world?" _____
What is the approximate time period during which this warning was given? _____

3. What is the corner stone of the church? _____

4. What is the mission of the remnant church? _____
_____
_____
_____

5. What are the three angel's messages? _____
_____
_____

6. What are the five testimonies of a true prophet? _____
_____
_____

7. Why is a revival of sanctuary study now due? _____
_____
Cite two Biblical references to support your answer. _____

Chapter 34: *The Church of the Temple Eternal—The Church of the Firstborn*

1. What takes place after the work of the remnant church has been completed? _____

2. Who are the members of the church of the Firstborn? _____

3. What will be the mission of the church of the Firstborn during the first 1000 years in heaven?_____
   What will be their occupation(s) in subsequent years _____

4. Describe how God has put His seal, the Sabbath, on each generation of the church.

   1. _____
   2. _____
   3. _____
   4. _____

Chapter 35: *Christ Coming for His Bride*

1. What is the Lambs' bride or wife? Is it the city, the New Jerusalem, or is it the redeemed saints, or both?
   _____

2. What constellation, whose depth cannot be measured, has fascinated and puzzled astronomers?
   _____

3. All the inhabitants of heaven will be present to welcome the "joyous homecoming of the redeemed." On what two other occasions did representatives from the unfallen worlds assemble in heaven?
   _____

Chapter 36: *"The Marriage of the Lamb"*

1. What are the four celebrations of redemption? _____
   _____

2. What is the significance of the rainbow round about the throne? _____
   _____

3. What are the seven anthems or songs that comprise the seven-part oratorio? _____
   _____

Chapter 37: *The Verdict of Jehovah's Jury*

1. "At the end of the _____ years when the _____ of the _____ is finished, Christ again returns to this _____ to _____ His _____ _____ and _____ the _____ from _____."

2. What are the four different verdicts handed down by Jehovah's jury? _____ _____, _____, _____, and _____

3. Name the three coronations of Christ _____, _____, _____, _____

Chapter 38: *The Temple Eternal—Its Most Holy Place*

1. "Will there be a temple after redemption?" _____ What Bible reference supports your answer? _____

2. What happened to the Garden of Eden, the tree of life and the tree of the knowledge of good and evil?

3. "What is the function of the most holy place of the temple eternal"? _____

Chapter 39: *The Temple Eternal—Its Holy Place*

1. What do each of the seven pillars upholding the temple of wisdom represent? _____, _____, _____, _____, _____, _____, and _____

2. "The _____ of the _____, that is _____: and to _____ from _____ is _____" Job 28:28.

3. What will be some of the courses of study in the New Earth University? _____

Chapter 40: *The Temple Eternal—Its Court*

1. What is the one trace "of the great Sacrifice, as a memorial to the redeemed throughout eternity of what their salvation has cost"? _____

2. What are some of the "no more" in the new earth? _____

3. "Christ is also the great center of the _____ sanctuary; in its holy place He is our _____ High Priest and the _____ _____ _____: in the most holy where He now officiates, He is our righteous _____. In heaven itself, He is _____ _____ _____ _____ _____ _____ _____."

   "He is _____ _____ to the _____ _____ GOD." (p.269)

ANSWER KEY

Chapter 1

1. creation, sanctuary, Bible

2. The plan of salvation

3. "in our study and teaching of nature, the work of Christ not only as **Creator** but as **Redeemer**, is made plain."

4. "Thus, the sanctuary not only illuminates **truth**, but it reveals **errors**."

5. **Bible, After the sacrificial lamb met its antitype in the death of the Lamb of God**

Chapter 2

1. Moses, through the sanctuary and its services

2. "Through **Christ** was to be fulfilled the purpose of which the **tabernacle** was a symbol" (Ed 36).

3. Psalm 29:9 (margin) states that "**in His temple every whit of it uttereth His glory**."

4. Exodus – Christ our Sanctuary
   Leviticus – Christ our Sacrifice
   Numbers – Christ our Guide
   Deuteronomy – Christ our Reward

5. "Through the **sanctuary** of the **Old Testament**, the gospel is presented in **type**; **the New Testament presents its antitype**."

Chapter 3

1. "A study of the sanctuary contains **spiritual food for all ages**."

2. "At the age of **twelve**, for the first time the child **Jesus** looked upon the **temple**.... The **mystery** of His **mission** was opening to the **Saviour**" (DA 78).

3. "that without a knowledge of **the sanctuary** 'it will be impossible for them (church members) to exercise **the faith** which is essential at this time, or to occupy the **position** God designs them to **fill**'".

4. "The **sanctuary** illustrates not only the plan of **salvation** in general, but it points out the **great gospel truths** that pertain particularly to **our own time** and on **down** to the very **end of time**."

5. "In the **future**, **deception** of every kind is to arise, and we want **solid ground** for our feet. The **enemy** will bring in **false theories** that there is **no sanctuary**. This is one of the points on which there will be a **departure** from the **faith**" (Ellen G. White, RH, May 25, 1905).

Chapter 4

1. 430 years sojourning - Exod. 12:40 and 400 years of bondage – Gen. 15:13

2. Yes or No

3. Sabbath

4. "The **earthly sanctuary** was to be a '**pattern** of the things in the heavens'" (Heb. 9:23).

5. sapphire stone
   Blue indicated obedience to heavenly truth (Numb. 15:36-40)

Chapter 5

1. "Let them make Me a sanctuary that I may dwell among them."
2. a place set apart for a sacred purpose
3. "Behold the tabernacle (dwelling place) of God is with men, and He will dwell with them, and they shall be His people, and God Himself shall be with them, and be their God".

Chapter 6

1. "Our **attitude** toward **Sabbath observance** determines **whether we stand under the black banner of the prince of the power of the air, or under the bloodstained banner of Prince Emmanuel.**"
2. "The **amount** has nothing to do with **true giving**."
3. Recompense for unpaid labor from the Egyptians

Chapter 7

1. "God puts **wisdom** in 'all who are **wise hearted**', that is, all who from the **heart dedicate** their **talents** to Him."
2. "which the **hand**, the **head**, and the **heart**, received **symmetrical attention**. It was a **pattern** for all time."
3. God
4. "Every man also to whom God hath given **riches**, and **wealth**, and hath given him **power** to **eat** thereof, and to take his portion, and to **rejoice** in his **labor**; this is the **gift of God**."
5. "There is no **limit** to the **usefulness** of one who, putting **self aside**, makes room for the **working** of the **Holy Spirit** upon his heart, and lives a life **wholly consecrated** to God. All who consecrate **body**, **soul**, and **spirit** to His service will be constantly receiving a new endowment of **physical**, **mental**, and **spiritual** power."

Chapter 8

1. In the Garden of Eden
2. "Finally, the 'fullness of the time was come' (Gal 4:4), when the **Antitype** of the **sacrificial lamb** was to enter the **court of this earth**, when the **Son of God** was to lay aside **His divine glory** and **power** and take upon **Himself** the **weakness** of **sinful** flesh."
3. "His true **nature** and **mission** might have been clearly understood through a **spiritual** understanding of the **sanctuary** and the **prophecies**."

Chapter 9

1. the Court, the Holy Place, the Most Holy Place
2. purity/righteousness, sacrifice, royalty, obedience
3. "As the **gate** was the way, and the **only** way to the **sanctuary court**, so **Christ** is the only way to **heaven**."

Chapter 10

1. "The cross of **Christ**, represented in the **altar**, is the center of **Christ's** life and of the **Christian's** life on **earth**; the **throne**, represented in the **ark**, is the center of **His life** in **heaven** and of the **Christian's** future life in heaven."

2. "Brass signifies **strength**, **stability**, **endurance**, and **victory** through suffering."

3. "In the **sanctuary**, silver represents **redemption through Christ**."

Chapter 11

1. a lamb-without blemish, a male of the first year
   This Lamb represented Christ.

2. "As **brass** represented **suffering**, so the **altar** as a whole was a symbol of **Christ** and Him **crucified**."

3. "Christ was treated as we **deserve**, that we might be treated as He **deserves**" (DA 25).

4. "Those who **surrender** their **lives** to His **guidance** and to His **service** will never be placed in a **position** for which He has not made **provision**" (MH 248, 249.

5. "The fact that we are called upon to **endure trials** shows that the **Lord Jesus** sees in us something **precious**, which He desires to **develop**" (MH 471).

Chapter 12

1. The laver was located between the altar and the door of the Holy Place.
   It was made of polished brass mirrors.

2. Baptism and feet washing

3. "The laver is the complement of the **altar**; that is, **reconciliation**, the work begun at the **altar**, is completed in **justification** symbolized at the **laver**."

Chapter 13

1. Fine white linen of woven work; whole and without blemish.

2. Righteousness

3. "The **material** and **simplicity** of the priests' **garments** betokened also the beauty of **character** of every **Christian** who is an **ambassador** for **Christ**."

4. Patriarchal Period (Adam—Jacob), Deliverance from Egypt (tribe of Levi), Ascension of Christ (Christ—High Priest)

Chapter 14

1. Bells of gold and pomegranates of blue, and purple, and scarlet, and twined linen.

2. Names of the tribes of Israel

3. HOLINESS TO THE LORD

Chapter 15

1. "The **earthly** sanctuary is important because it was God's **object lesson** to illustrate **redemption** in the **heavenly**."

2. "Moreover, since the plan of **salvation** is the '**grand central theme**' of the Bible, an understanding of both the **earthly** and the **heavenly sanctuary** is fundamental to a proper understanding of the **Bible**."

3. "A **clear** and **definite** picture of the **sanctuary** above will enable us to follow **Christ** where He is now **ministering** for the **salvation** of man."

Chapter 16

1. Psalms

2. Passover, Lord's Supper

3. The Holy Spirit

Chapter 17

1. It means we have now enlisted in God's army; we are His soldiers, volunteers in a lifelong warfare, with Christ and Satan as opposing generals.

2. "**Justification**, obtained in the court, is our **passport** into the **Holy Place**."

3. "While **justification**--the second birth--is the work of a **moment**; **sanctification**, this 'growing up' process, is the work of a **lifetime**, the result of battles fought, and victories won."

Chapter 18

1. twice as high

2. shittim wood—wild acacia of the desert

3. gold, silver

Chapter 19

1. fine-twined linen, white goats' hair, rams' skins dyed red, and badgers' skins

2. burnt offering, peace offering, consecration offering, trespass offering, and wave offering

3. Lowly Saviour, sacrificial Saviour, sinless Saviour, and exalted Saviour

Chapter 20

1. "The **table** provides our **first opportunity** for **Christian** growth for **character perfection**--for **sanctification**."

2. Jesus
   John 6:35, John 6: 32, John 6:33, John 6:38

3. fine flour, oil, salt, and water

Chapter 21

1. Prayer—altar of prayer

2. stacte/myrrh, onycha, galbannum, and frankincense

3. unbelief, selfishness, willful disobedience, an evil heart, irreverence, and an unforgiving spirit

Chapter 22

1. light-bearing--candlestick

2. almonds hasten to put forth new blossoms, they represent new life in Christ, and they mean "wakeful"

3. "While **imputed** righteousness frees us from the **penalty** of our **past sins**, **imparted** righteousness frees us **day** by **day** from the **power** of sin, and gives us '**power** to become the sons of God' John (**1:12**)"

Chapter 23

1. Daniel 9:24, 27
   Daniel 8:14; 7:10

2. 457 BC
   Daniel 9:25, and Ezra 7
   the cleansing of the heavenly sanctuary, the judgment of the "house of God"
   AD 1844 (Daniel 8:14)

3. the time when Christ would give His life a ransom for the world
   the time when He would begin the judgment of the "house of God"

4. Jesus

Chapter 24

1. sanctification

2. We must follow Christ where He leads the way…to accept the judgment message of Revelation 14:7-12 and to walk in all the light.
   Cleansing Room, Glory Room

Chapter 25

1. Ark—a place of safety or refuge
   Noah's ark and Jochebed's ark for baby Moses

2. Within its heart rested His law, His special treasure.

3. the tables of the covenant (10 commandments), a pot of manna, and Aaron's rod

Chapter 26

1. God's throne

2. Jehovah

3. the foundation of His throne

Chapter 27

1. Silver was a symbol of redemption.
   Trumpets "of one whole piece" were to remind the people at this solemn time, their thoughts were to be centered on preparation for the Day of Atonement.

2. The day of God's judgment for the human race, when every individual will either be separated from his sins or cut off from the heavenly family is the antitype of the Day of Atonement.
   The Day of Atonement
   AD 1834

3. a holy convocation, afflict the soul, offer an offering, and do no work

4. abstain and fast
   "For whatsoever soul it be that shall not be afflicted in that same day, he shall be cut off from among his people" Lev. 23:29.

5. "There was to be no **divided heart**, —the day of **Atonement** demanded **complete** and **wholehearted consecration** of every **power**."

Chapter 28

1. "The **Sabbath** was set apart to be **kept** in **honor** of God's **holy name**" (EW33).

2. Name of person in authority – "Lord thy God"
   Title – Creator (Maker)
   Territory – "Heaven and earth, the sea, and all that in them is"
   "Lord thy God," Creator (Maker), and "Heaven and earth, the sea, and all that in them is"

3. The antediluvians had strong memories and transmitted the law unimpaired to their posterity, then God engraved it in tables of stone that it might not be forgotten, and later the law was recorded in the complete Bible.

Chapter 29

1. book of life, book of remembrance, and book of sins

2. sins

3. Am I ready? Are you ready? Get ready! Get ready! Get ready!

Chapter 30

1. "The **order** so strikingly **displayed** in all works of God was **manifest** in the **Hebrew economy**… At Sinai, the arrangements for **organization** were completed" (Ed37).

2. myrrh, cinnamon, calamus, and cassia

3. A type of setting up and anointing of the heavenly sanctuary, "the Most Holy" which took place at the ascension of Christ and was explained in Daniel 9:21, 24.

Chapter 31

1. Hebrew generation, Christian church, remnant church, and church of the firstborn/finally redeemed.

2. Hebrew church
   The first step in the organization of the Hebrew church was the giving of a "constitution," a fundamental law which expressed "the whole duty of man," and by which all should be guided.

3. To teach the idolatrous nations around them of the true and living God that inhabiteth eternity, and of the holy and just and eternal character of His law, His oracle.

Chapter 32

1. "Go ye…and teach all nations…to observe all things whatsoever I have commanded you," "beginning in Jerusalem."

2. Faith in Christ as the Son of God, the Saviour of the world.

3. the Great Reformation exposed deceptive errors, and the Bible translated and made accessible to common people

Chapter 33

1. "that which is left after a part has been removed:"

2. "The hour of His judgement is come."
   AD 1834

3. The sanctuary

4. proclamation of the prophecies concerning the judgment and Christ's second coming, an understanding of the sanctuary and its relation to the law of God; and to rescue these truths from their companionship with errors, and reset them in the framework of truth

5. the judgment and Sabbath message, a warning to come out of Babylon, the command not to worship the beast and his image and to identify with God's commandment keepers and those with the faith of Jesus

6. emphasize the truths of the judgment, the sanctuary, the Sabbath "according to the commandments", the signs of Christ's second coming, and the everlasting gospel in its original purity

7. Before the end, the sanctuary is to be "restored to its rightful position."
   Daniel 8:14 and Amos 9:11

Chapter 34

1. The Investigative judgement--judgment of the house of God closes.

2. Those whose names are written by the Father in the Book of Life. "A great multitude which no man could number" Rev. 7:9. Those who are redeemed by the blood of Christ.

3. "The saints shall judge the world" 1 Cor. 6:2
   varied occupations, students in the school of the hereafter

4. Hebrew – founded on God's law, the seal—the Sabbath—1500 BC
   Christian—Holy Spirit sent to believers—AD 31
   Remnant—Sabbath divinely revealed and restored—AD 1844
   Firstborn—Second coming of Christ—continue to observe commandment—Isa. 66:23

Chapter 35

1. It is both. See Rev. 21:2, 9, 10—Uriah Smith comments (Daniel and Revelation, p. 733)

2. Orion

3. when the foundation of the earth was laid (Job 38:6, 7) and when Christ broke the fetters of the tomb (The Desire of Ages, pp. 833-834)

Chapter 36

1. when Christ entered the court of earth to become our Sacrifice as the Babe of Bethlehem, when He entered the Holy Place of the heavenly sanctuary to be our High Priest, when He entered the Most Holy Place within the second veil to act as Judge, and after the close of probation, "the marriage of the Lamb"

2. The rainbow is the emblem of Christ's everlasting covenant of peace with the redeemed—an assurance that God is true. It is a pledge that God will keep all His promises of salvation to those who have put their trust in Him.

3. the Anthem of the Four Living Creatures, the Song of the Four and Twenty Elders, the Song of the 144,000, the Song of the "Great Multitude", the Hallelujah Chorus, the "Amen" sung by the angels, and the Father's Solo

Chapter 37

1. "At the end of the **thousand** years when the **judgment** of the wicked is finished, Christ again returns to this **earth** to **execute** His **righteous judgment** and **cleanse** the **earth** from **sin**."

2. the verdict of the unfallen worlds, the verdict of the redeemed, the verdict of the universe, and the verdict completed

3. KING OF GLORY, KING OF KINGS AND LORD OF LORDS, KING OF ETERNITY

Chapter 38

1. Yes
   Ezek. 37:25-27

2. God transplanted them to paradise above—to the Most Holy Place of the temple eternal.

3. The Most Holy Place is the seat of God's universal government, the scene of special occasions for the redeemed, the location for the marriage and marriage supper of the lamb, the site of the final coronation of Christ, and the assembling place for divine worship.

Chapter 39

1. knowledge, understanding, judgment, equity, discretion, prudence, and justice

2. "The **fear** of the **Lord**, that is **wisdom**: and to **depart** from **evil** is **understanding**" Job 28:28.

3. the universe, nature, the glories of the heavens, the innumerable worlds, the human body, science history, music and song, God's creative power, God's redemptive power…

Chapter 40

1. Jesus has "horns coming out of his hand; bright beams out of His side," "and there was the hiding of His power" (Hab. 3:4).

2. animal sacrifices, sin, trouble, sickness, disabilities, death, loneliness, financial worries, hunger, different languages…

3. "Christ is also the great center of the **heavenly** sanctuary; in its holy place He is our **sympathizing** High Priest and the **KING OF GLORY**: in the most holy where He now officiates, He is our righteous **Judge**. In heaven itself, He is **KING OF KINGS AND LORD OF LORDS**."

    "He is **THE PATH** to the **THRONE OF** GOD." (p.269)

www.ingramcontent.com/pod-product-compliance
Lightning Source LLC
Chambersburg PA
CBHW081352040426
42450CB00015B/3406